GENERATION WHY

SUSAN BOHNET

SMIRK BOOKS

INTRODUCTION

In our families we find our greatest joys. It is also where we find our greatest killjoys. And maybe it was meant to be this way. If family life were always rosy, we might not appreciate it. It's all about the highs and lows.

**Sweet angelic children opposed to the wild devilish variety. (Same children--different amount of shut-eye)

**Helpful sweet children opposed to defiant, wilful ones. (Again, same kids--different mood of the moment.)

**Milk in a glass opposed to milk on a kitchen table. (Different milk--very, very different.)

Young children seem to find their way into an amazing amount of trouble without trying. Of course, they wouldn't try. They are sweet kids. I think a parent's greatest skill is the ability to see what's happening in the moment and figuratively step back and say, "Someday, this will be funny."

There is that flicker, no more than a moment, between observing the conditions and choosing how to react. Everything swings in the balance. Fed up or forbearance, anger or amusement? It's a monumental millisecond.

As Mom comes upon her daughter with expensive face cream spread up and down her little legs and into the bath mat on which she sits, a few things happen in quick succession. Mom's breath catches in her throat. She calculates the cost of the cream oozing between the little toes. She calculates the age those toes will appear by tomorrow with the miraculous anti-aging qualities the cream boasts. The vein above her right eye pounds like the little drummer boy is going to town on it--the little drummer boy covered in eight per cent alpha hydroxy, retinol facial smoother. Then it's there, the moment of reaction. The eyebrows on her forehead fight with each other--down in anger or up in amusement. They quiver, turn into a unibrow, separate and pull up the corners of her mouth. Much of the cream will be lost but she salvages what she can; what's a little toe jam from a sweet two-year-old? Score one for Mom.

A tendril of smoke finds it's way heavenward from behind the rocking chair. Dad spots it and leaps from the couch. His soldering iron is plugged into the outlet and lies unattended. There is a hole burned through the carpet...and the underlay. Even the strand board beneath has an active area of black spreading on it. How did this happen? He certainly didn't leave it plugged in? "Oh, would you look at that?" says his son behind him with a soccer ball under one arm. "I plugged it in but it didn't look like it was doing anything so I just put it down." Dad's moment has arrived. He sucks in his breath. He imagines the catastrophe that was narrowly avoided. He calculates the cost of replacing the living room carpet, and wonders if a throw rug in this semi-obscure area would do. The vein above his eye pounds with the veracity of a muscle car engine. His jaw is clenched. He takes a breath. "Don't plug things in and walk away," he manages to say. "It can be dangerous." Score one for Dad.

Once the moments pass--and they eventually do--these stories will come up at family get-togethers for years to come. And when these kids become parents themselves, they will truly appreciate the strength that was demonstrated.

Those stressful times can eat away at our sanity or give us a good laugh. If, that is, we decide we'd rather laugh than moan. Moaning has its place. I won't completely knock moaning. You can vent a lot of frustration with a forceful moan. But, moans that dissolve into giggles before too long are best. You may prefer to skip straight to the laughter, however. Good choice. Laughing burns more calories per minute.

Parents have many responsibilities. We really need down time to recharge. I find that one good smile is as good as a zap from a jumper cable. (And I'm not particularly adept at attaching jumper cables, so I know.)

In the grand scheme of things, that hole in the living room carpet won't mean much--I'm still chanting that one to myself, daily.

I hope you will find relaxation, perspective, and someone (you and me) to chuckle at in the pages of this book. You are a parent, accepting and embracing the greatest role in history, without prior training. There are going to be glitches along the way. And you are hereby granted permission to smirk.

PART I

MIND YOUR P'S AND Q'S

MIND YOUR P'S AND Q'S

~

*H*aving a family is wonderful, but it is also a frenzied life. When I used to tell people I had three children under five they would look faint and say, "I guess you're going to be busy!" Now that I have five children, most people can't even articulate their thoughts. They simply stammer and take a step back in case it's catching.

As a new mother, I had a plan. At three months, my son would excuse himself when he burped, even if I was patting his back at the time. At six months, he would be potty trained and would discretely flaunt it at social gatherings. "Please wash behind my ears" and "Thank you for the strained liver" would be common phrases around our house. Algebra would be mastered at one and....Well, you get the picture.

When my husband and I had the third child, an amazing thing happened. They out-numbered us. They had a majority. They took over. My goals became much more realistic:

1. Make it through the day without popping a blood vessel in my forehead. (I sometimes had to send myself to my room to accomplish this one.)

2. If a child is running with a butcher knife, make sure the pointy end is down.

3. One plus one equals teasing of the third, so if children gather in the basement, close the door and turn up the T.V.

I still insisted on basic politeness and correct grammar, however. Then one day I heard my eldest son say to the younger, "Your Ninja Turtle guys *is* choking on their own blood." I quickly corrected him, "That's 'your Ninja Turtle guys *are* choking on their own blood,' Honey." I then had a mental flash twenty years into the future of a very polite axe murderer correcting the judge, "Five bodies *are* in the sewer."

I knew I'd have to expand my goals. It was time for minding not just the P's and the Q's but the whole sordid alphabet. It looks like I *am* going to be busy!

GENERATION WHY

~

I don't know who gets to name a generation Baby Boomers or Generation X or Generation Y. My children are certainly part of the Y group.

"Why, why, why," that's all I ever hear. "Why is the sky blue? Why can't we have another freezie? Why am I the only one to get mosquito bites? Why do your eyes look like they are going to pop out of your head when I spill milk?" The questions are endless.

My kids have always had an insatiable curiosity for reasons. Even as a very small child, my oldest discovered the word that would fill his mind with knowledge and his mother with stress. I perched over the bassinet and cooed, "Come on Darling, say 'Mommy.'" He looked up at me with dark brown eyes full of wonder and said, "Why?"

I was flabbergasted. "Well, because," I said. "I'm your Mommy and you are going to have to call me sometime when you need something."

The child was smarter than that. All he had to do was cry and Mommy was there in a matter of seconds.

I tried another approach. "It would make Mommy very happy to hear you say her name." He smiled sweetly and spit up on his blanket and sleeper. Then he messed his pants. Making Mommy happy was obviously not high on the child's list of priorities. Soon the child realized that knowing my name did hold certain advantages. Such as getting my attention, so he could ask me more *Why* questions.

As time passed, the child's questioning ability really picked up speed. "Why does blood come out of my nose when I fall down? Why does cheese get furry when I leave it in my closet too long? Why do you rub your temples so much?" These and many other questions were learned quickly by my first Generation Why child. The siblings who followed were under his tutelage.

Lately, their favorite question is, "What is there to eat?" My sweet little bottomless pits are asking for snacks before they finish chewing the last bites of their dinner.

There is one question, however, that the children have truly mastered. If there were an Olympic event in asking it, they would all be crammed there together on the top platform. The question is "Why do I have to go to bed?" This question has been asked in enough variations to keep a child of three up until 11:45.

All the reports I've heard from parents suggest that the Generation Whys become more adept questioners as they age. Soon I'll be expecting to answer, "Why can't I stay out 'till four in the morning?" I hope I do a little better than I did getting my son to say "Mommy" or I could really be in for some late nights.

COMPLICATED OR CHILD'S PLAY

~

*C*hildren play in a carefree and light-hearted manner. At least, that's the misconception among parents. And a pleasant misconception it is. I'd like to stay contentedly immersed in that school of thought.

Unfortunately, I am often called upon to mediate: Like yesterday, the little girl pointed at her brother and said, "He was the puppy and now he's a cat! Tell him he has to be the puppy."

It was an outrage. No one authorized this metamorphosis.

Another time, someone said, "Mom, I'm a monster! And I'm always the monster; I'm tired of it." Who could blame her? Friends continually fleeing from your presence gets old fast. These are my involvements with child's play. And it's as far as I want to go.

I recently saw a title in a ladies magazine that said, "Helping your child become a successful player." Do I need to be an active participant when they play with peers?

Should I give monster-acting tips? "Let that growl come from the diaphragm. And see what you can do with a little phlegm in the back of your throat. That's it."

I don't know why we have to analyze our children's playing talents at all. From the stories I hear, the previous generation's parents were content that the kids were off playing and they were given some blessed peace. Now we want to know what they're playing and what their play indicates about their future.

Do I need to study up on my role? Do I need "advice for the play coach"? Do the children need a play coach? I can't believe that it gets any more complicated than, "Don't pull your friend's hair or she might not come back tomorrow."

But people like to study things...so let's.

Let's look at imaginary friends. Can you see them? And if you do, does that mean you will have talents with the unseen and be the type to pronounce, "This house is clean?" Or does it mean you are creatively gifted? Or does it just mean you have an imaginary friend?

What if my child is bossy? The article I read suggested that a child with difficulty giving up control may grow up to be a great leader. Well, I suppose that's a possibility. So are the chances that he'll one day be voted, "Most likely to get a fist in the chops."

I must admit; I did become concerned with the children's play on one occasion. I found several decapitated Barbie dolls. Much to my daughter's horror, I couldn't get the heads back on properly. She wasn't concerned with what her brothers had done to them, just that the dolls might have to stay that way. The boys were equally upset that the heads were permanently removed. They were just playing. (I have since heard that a beheaded Barbie can be fixed. Is it true? Can you re-capitate a Barbie? I threw away six Barbie dolls.)

I may be shirking my responsibility, but I'm not going to interfere in child's play unless the wailing of one of the children drags me in. I, like my forefathers and mothers, am just grateful for that blessed peace when they are off quietly playing. As long as they're not playing too quietly, that is. Everyone knows that means the worst trouble of all. Inevitably someone emerges with a bald spot or an empty bottle of nail polish.

THE COVETED SPOT ON THE CHROMOSOME

~

*S*ome things go hand in hand. You just don't seem to find one without the other, like peanut butter and jelly. Those two are basically inseparable. During the school year, I go into high peanut butter and jelly making mode. It is such a favorite with my children that once my young son couldn't remember the word "lunch" so he said, "That meal we always have peanut butter at." Other things go together as well: alarm clocks and groaning, 8:15 am and insanity, insanity and premature greying.

Scientists might not be able to prove the insanity-grey hair link but they have made an interesting discovery. You are four times more likely to have thinning bones if you went grey early. I read that a Dr. Clifford J. Rosen believes these genes are close together and that's why they are acting in sync.

We are making strides in genetic research. Now, what is most vitally needed is a way to rearrange the genes. If we could regroup the genes, not only could we get that grey hair gene away from the bone density gene, we could ensure our children's academic success.

All we would have to do is place the gene responsible for video game addiction smack-dab against the algebra gene. That would give that algebra gene a jump-start like nothing else. Kids would come home complaining that they only have 32 questions of algebra homework and couldn't we find them an extra practice workbook somewhere. Please. Parents would have to set timers and say, "You can only do algebra until the timer goes off, then you'll have to watch a little TV or something."

We could arrange the genes so that the language appreciation gene is beside the "I want to look cool" gene. Children will come home begging for 'The Complete Works of William Shakespeare' in leather bound covers. "Come on Mom, all the kids are getting them." Soon they will be reporting that so-and-so has a copy of War and Peace, and the guy down the street claims to appreciate Ernest Hemingway. They will lament their own sparse personal libraries. For Christmas, they will plead for books and more books, no electronic gadgets or name-brand clothing for them. They just wouldn't be able to show their face in public without a critically acclaimed book...the thicker and more challenging the better.

Perhaps the most powerful and the most coveted places on the chromosome strand are either side of the music fan gene. I have reserved those spots for physics and chemistry. Though it may be unfamiliar to their parents, soon children will be quoting Einstein's Theory of Relativity at the dinner table. They will discuss the thrill of combining sodium (Na) and a simple little chlorine atom (Cl) and arriving at such a tasty result...(NaCl)...salt. Things will go a little further for those children with an especially active music fan gene, you know, the kind of gene that inspires children to sleep on sidewalks to get tickets to concerts and then scream over the music the whole time. These kids will insist on doing their hair in the extreme flyaway style of Einstein, himself. They will hang test tubes and Bunsen burners from their belt loops. Parents will roll their eyes, and enroll them in extra credit courses.

But even without a rearrangement of the genes, studying and good grades will always go hand in hand...so until that blessed genetic rearranging is available the old rule will have to stand: no video games until homework is done.

FIRST STEPS ON THE CAREER PATH

~

I'd like to know what goes on at recess. I used to toboggan down the school hill as long as the snow and ice lasted. Others made snow angels. The confrontational children made snow forts complete with ammunition. I don't think my boys are doing any of these things. Why don't I just ask them what they do at recess? I do. They say they are 'playing.' That's as specific as it gets. If I want to know the nitty-gritty, I must, therefore, turn to circumstantial evidence. There are strange clues. I'm sure the answers are there, if only I could make sense of them.

I suspect that my boys are receiving a valuable education during recess. From what I can tell, recess is kind of like work experience or some sort of practicum.

The commerce practicum perfects the child's wheeling-dealing skills. First, I found pretty little cardboard disks in his coat pocket. "Those are Pogs," he said. He launched into an enthusiastic explanation that went into far too great detail. And truthfully, I spaced off after the part where an unfortunate bang of the "slammer" could mean the loss of all a player's pogs, but it seemed the real thrill was in the trading. "Look at how cool this one is," my child said as he held up a pog with a metallic-looking skull and crossbones on it. "I traded a dolphin pog for it. I got a deal."

Not long afterward, I asked to see the cool skull pog. The child knit his eyebrows together. "Mom, pogs are out," he said as though I had asked to see a butter churn.

"What's in?" I asked.

"Pokemon cards!" He then pulled out a stack of trading cards with little animals and energy signs on them. "Pikachu is my favorite. Today I traded Manchop and Sandshrew for Charmander; he's rare."

"Are you getting second language credits for this?"

"You've got to know when to trade. It's all in the timing."

Before long the Pokemon cards were no longer in. "What's the new cool collector's items?" I asked recently.

"Nothing, really," he said. "The market is sluggish."

I put my arm around his shoulder and led him to the newspaper. "My son, let me introduce you to the stock market. I wonder if gold is up."

My other son is undoubtedly doing road construction over the recess break. The child wears holes in his mittens that cannot be explained in any other way. He is on his third pair of mittens this winter. The jackhammer is the only viable explanation.

When the recess bell rings, he must pull on his toque and mittens and meet the road crew on the back lane. The foreman drops a hard hat over his head and asks, "How was Math?"

"Okay," he says and shoves the burly man out of the way. Holding tightly to the jackhammer, even his extra thick mittens take a beating. Then, when he sees the other children begin to run back into the school, he deduces that the bell has rung (his own ears unable to hear over the racket). He lays down the power tool. "I'll be back as soon as I finish my peanut butter sandwich," he calls over his shoulder.

Maybe I should have been more resourceful with my own recess time. I feel like a slacker. Tobogganing and snow angel making are such childish pursuits.

SNOWMEN FOR SALE

~

The snowman is a cheery sight. Mounds of fluffy snow are rolled with glee and piled one on top of another. Through the winter months, making snowmen has been a favorite children's pastime for generations. "Frosty the Snowman" has danced across my television screen every winter for as long as I can remember. However, my son has taken the pastime to new commercial heights.

He called me outside yesterday to parade his product. In his little mitten-clad hands he held a perfectly shaped, two-foot tall, snowman. My other children and the neighbor boy, Billy, bounced up and down in their boots with excitement. "We're going to sell them!" they announced. "But you can have one for free."

"Thanks," I said, and then I tried to control the corners of my mouth but found the task monumental, so I said, "Good luck," and hurried into the kitchen to grin at the salad I was preparing.

Within a couple of minutes, the air rang with the call, "Look Mom!" With such overwhelming joy that he forgot to remove his boots before running through the house, my son held up a shiny penny. "Billy's Mom bought one!" he beamed.

His penny was zipped into his coat pocket for safekeeping and he hurried out to play. Or so I thought. Play was not on his mind...work was!

The younger children performed their assembly line tasks as the eldest, the foreman, directed operations. In record time they had five more mini-snowmen. The entire group descended on the next-door neighbor's step for a high-pressure sale. And on they went down the block.

Soon they were back in our front yard. "How's it going?" I asked.

"We've got to fix it. The head fell off this one." Quality control...that is always a concern once a business starts to grow.

By dinnertime, they had sold two snowmen. Apparently, Billy's Mom was so thrilled with her first snowman, she was eager to buy another.

It was a great business. They enjoyed their work. They had some exercise. They got plenty of fresh air. But most importantly, the two cents they had earned was pure profit. The free snow in our front yard was not likely to dwindle. And if it did there was always the backyard. There were no hassles with middlemen over varying costs of raw materials to hinder their business. Not only that, no labor negotiations were necessary since the entire workforce was unaware of the value of a penny, and thus willing to work for sheer enjoyment alone.

My little entrepreneur was off and running. Cash flow issues were anticipated. A substantial loan was procured to cover making change. Then he ran into a snag. Reality. With a goal of $126.95 to cover the cost of the Lego set he wanted he wouldn't have enough, even if he sold a snowman to everyone in town.

"I need something I can sell for more money," he determined. "How much do you think I could get for an igloo?"

THE THREE BEANS

~

*M*oms are mean. Especially those who don't mean to be. In the effort to keep the child properly nourished, we set ourselves up for bitter resistance. Our goals are not appreciated. The child does not look at the long-range effects of eating green beans. He cannot comprehend the complexities of the human body at the cellular level. The connection between a bean and the nutrients that the body needs to be healthy and strong is not made. All he knows is that he'd rather have a chocolate chip cookie. If we could only get inside each other's minds perhaps some understanding could take place.

Mom's Mind: Green beans are a vegetable. Health professionals suggest multiple servings of vegetables and fruit. Green beans will fill a portion of that requirement. Therefore, I will cook beans tonight.

Oh, would you look at that? They're just sitting there on his plate. He must consume the beans before they will do him any good. It's too bad. It would make my life much easier if serving the "serving" would do the trick.

Mom says: "You're not leaving your chair until you eat at least three of those beans. I don't care if you don't like them; they're good for you." Then, while Mom is holding three beans on the child's fork, "Open your mouth. Open it. There. Don't you dare spit that out! Oh, stop it. Get that look off your face. They're good. For heavens sakes, what a fuss you make over three little beans."

Meanwhile across the table in the....

Child's Mind: Uh oh. What's that? Does she think I'm going to eat that stuff? She always makes those yucky green things. She is so mean. She never makes anything I like. I looked in the fridge and cupboards. There's lots of good stuff, but she never makes dinner out of the good stuff. We have Oreos and ice cream. Why couldn't we have that for dinner? And there are popcorn and raisins and chocolate chips in the pantry. Those would be good. What's she saving them for? After I'm in bed?

Gross. She put those beans on my plate. One is even touching my spaghetti. Now I can't eat that, either.

If she gets that fork any closer to my mouth, I'm going to die. Oh, I can smell them. All three beans in my mouth at once! It's too much to chew!

Child says: "Nooooo. I don't like them. They're too squishy. They're too smelly. They're too green." (Gag -- swallow) "Meany."

Mom concludes: There, now you'll be healthy and have the energy to run... "Hey, where do you think you're going? Come back here. You haven't even touched your spaghetti."

Despite the unrewarding nature of this responsibility, the mother will continue to try to feed the child healthy food, thinking one day he will understand. However, this could be the child who will, one day, write the sequel to Mommie Dearest. And the truth of the matter is that on that day, as he's hunched over his computer writing all sorts of disparaging things, he will be healthy enough to write his book for the sole reason that his mother made him eat three green beans when he was five.

RHAPSODY ON A THEME OF GOIN' PEE PEE

~

*F*ew endeavors require more creativity than
potty training. You may doubt, thinking that
such ventures as painting, sculpting or even writing
symphonies requires more creative energy. Not so. Potty
training is the true test of creative talent.

I try to make potty training as entertaining as possible.
When the child performs the desired act, the entire family
yells, "Yahoo!" We also jump up and down and clap our
hands. My older daughters even break into a potty song
they have written just for the occasion. No matter where
the family may be in the house, the word is spread, and we
all cheer the youngster for her accomplishment. She should
love the attention, the praise, and the admiration so much
that she will do whatever it takes to get it again.
Unfortunately, the child has very healthy self-esteem and
doesn't require praise often.

Another potty training variation involves a good-time-
had-by-all. We keep up the "Yahooing" and encourage the

child to join in all the fun. We dance and sing until the child is giddy with laughter. In theory, the child will have so much fun "goin' pee pee" that any other activity will pale by comparison. Watching videos, however, often takes precedence. In fact, the child suddenly views pulling up pants as an extremely cumbersome task. Excited parents coaxing the child to the bathroom with promises of fun are quickly dismissed with, "No, I want to see Simba."

Candy has its place. This is one of its places. Right after the Yahoo chorus, the child may be given anything she wants. We have Smarties, cookies, and chocolate chips. Bribery, you say? Tisk, tisk. I wouldn't say that. It's all in the wording. If I say to the child, "Mommy will give you a cookie if you go to the potty," then that could be construed as a bribe. If, however, I say, "Good job! You did it! You should get a little cookie for that," then what you have is a reward. A reward is nothing like a bribe, though the same cookie changes hands. It's an official "Rhapsody" loophole. (Go ahead; check the manual.)

About this time, the child realizes that she holds a wildcard. The 'wildcard variation' is basically potty overload. Going to the potty twelve times in a five-minute time span procures twelve cookies. Then around bedtime, she discovers the trump card--"I don't have to go to bed; I have to go potty." The child uses these cards indiscriminately. She's never had so much power. She will engage in battle to get to the bathroom. She also turns into a clean freak and spends excessive time with hand washing rituals. Anything to stay up!

Have you heard of the dolls that go potty? This is an interesting variation. The child potty trains the doll. Some parents say this works wonders. I wonder? I think this could be what is meant by, "Those who can, do; those who can't, teach."

There are books, magazine articles and even videos full of variations. Sigh. So what do you think, now? Rachmaninoff may disagree, but can you possibly believe that composing symphonies requires more creativity than variations on a theme of goin' pee pee? Well, it's a close call. One thing's for sure; I show much more rapture at the end of my rhapsody than his.

PART II

A BARRAGE OF BATTLES

THE PHONE FIGHT PHENOMENON

~

hat is it about a ringing telephone that sends children into a frenzy? They sit there calm as can be until the phone rings, then war breaks out. All five children begin fighting, screaming and demanding my undivided attention. One child suddenly has a fist-full of another's uprooted hair. Another child begins propelling porcelain ornaments at a sibling. And the baby suddenly stinks to high heaven.

People think I live in a mad house, which of course I do with five small children, but it's not as bad as it sounds via telephone. I get sympathetic expressions from some friends who wonder, "How do you make it through the day?" However, after hearing screams of torture coming over the telephone, one friend said, "My children don't scream that often." I matter-of-factly reminded her, "That's because you have one children and he doesn't fight with each other."

On those rare occasions when a massive brawl does not erupt the second I get on the phone, I become Ms. Popular. The children may have been playing happily for hours, but suddenly they all have matters of dire importance that must be discussed with me immediately.

Holding two conversations simultaneously is tricky at best. I thought I was getting pretty good at it, though. I could direct children to the paper towels so they could mop grape juice off the living room rug and hardly miss a beat in my conversation. However, I decided I would have to give this practice up after I once whispered to my youngest, "Let's do lunch," while I said to my friend, "I think you have a poopy diaper."

Now as my children try to talk to me, I say nothing...verbally that is. My facial muscles say all the kids need to know. I have mastered the art of giving *the look* while my voice doesn't reveal what my face is doing. My expression is saying, "Touch your brother again and you won't leave your room 'til you're thirty!" Meanwhile, my voice is saying, "That sounds lovely. I wish I could sew the way you do."

Even when you're not speaking though, it can be dangerous. You've really got to watch the body language. One wrong twitch of the head and you've agreed to have the entire neighborhood over for a water fight.

I've thought long and hard about this and I've come up with a plan that will solve everything. All I need is a telephone that, instead of the traditional ring, screams, "Bedtime!"

At the sound of "bedtime" children scatter. They begin their homework. They do the supper dishes. They have even been known to clean their bedrooms.

Yes, that kind of phone is really what I need. It would be the best invention since the pacifier. Besides the wonderful spin-off benefits that would occur, I could actually have a fightless phone call. Dare I dream?

TIC-TAC-WOES

~

I have heard of seats at an NFL game worth kicking the bucket over, cheesecake that's worth leaving this world for, and a balcony view worth jumping from to see. They were all described as "to die for." My children must figure that if these types of things are "to die for," a multitude of lesser items are at least worth "fighting for".

One thing worth fighting over is discarded packaging. My children will draw first blood over an empty cereal box...that is if someone else wants it. That seems to be the key. As long as one child wants to play with something, (be it a straw, a piece of plastic, or an old string), another child, seeing the pleasure derived from the soon-to-be garbage, will want it too. Desperately! Passionately! Violently!

We were visiting my hometown a few weeks ago when I became pointedly aware of how far my children will go. With the late nights we had been keeping visiting family, I knew my two-year-old would have a hard time sitting through church, so I brought a little candy along to keep her happy. The children all shared the candies quietly and uneventfully. The problem started when the candy was gone. They were not upset that there wasn't anymore. The candy did not cause the brawl that would soon break out. They were worried about who would get to play with the empty Tic-Tac box. There had been lots of candies. The candies were no thrill. But the box! There was only one box. And it wouldn't be fair if the two-year-old became the sole owner of the box. Why should she get it when everyone could see she was having so much fun with it? That joy should, rightly, be shared by all.

Something else my children believe worth fighting for is whether or not you get to be a frog or a lizard or a snake. I'm not sure exactly what the purpose of this game is or how they become these animals. However, I have never heard such heated debates over the pros and cons of each creature. And if one child firmly believes the frog to be the creature of choice, someone else had better not deny him his rightful metamorphosis.

The other day a child came to me in tears wailing, "He won't let me be a lizard!" Then through sobs she added, "He says I have to be the lizard's owner!"

How insulting! To expect her to be a human! Naturally, I had to become involved. As the mediator in the negotiations, it was my job to sit down with the parties involved and, with a straight face, ask, "Why can't she be a lizard?"

I can hardly blame my children for their warped sense of what is and isn't worth getting into a scrap over. They hear adults talking about cheesecake to die for, and certainly empty boxes and whether or not you are a lizard are more important than that.

CASH, CHARGE, AND CHILDREN

~

hen I was in high school I went shopping every Saturday. My friends and I would call each other up and say, "What time do you want to go?" There was never any confusion about "where"; that was understood. The only variance was our departure time.

We didn't have a lot of money to spend so we wanted to make an informed decision before forking over any hard-earned cash. I would try on the same dress every week for two months before I came up with the money to actually buy it. When we had finished the clothing store rounds, we went to the cafe for fries and gravy and serious discussions. "Yea, I know that dress is nice, but would it be the nicest thing I own? That's the real question. I have a date on Friday. I need to know these things."

My mom once asked me, "What did you do all afternoon?

"Nothing," I answered.

"Why did you go, then?"

"Something to do."

She found an inconsistency in doing nothing for something to do. You've just got to know how to do nothing properly, I guess.

These days I don't have time to do nothing when I go shopping. If I do go into a clothing store to browse, I am quickly reminded that children, especially boys, become bored with women's blouses before they even get to the rack. And that's on the first trip. There is no way I could take them to the blouse rack on a weekly basis. That would be a whine-wish if ever I've heard one.

Dealing with children's boredom in clothing stores is annoying but it's nothing compared to what a mother has to handle in grocery and drug stores. These stores may as well advertise, "Tantrums, or your money back." The tantrum seems to be the goal. Why else would they place chocolate bars, candy and gum three feet from the floor? It's not there to tempt my kneecaps. It's there to send my children, already tired from the shopping excursion, into a mouth-watering frenzy.

Thanks to this merciless marketing tactic, before the begging even begins I'm muttering, "No, nope, I said, 'not this time'."

We can't make it through the checkout without the children picking up at least seven different items. And in answer to each pair of hopeful eyes I say, "We already have treats at home. Please put it back. Didn't you hear me? Stop drooling on the wrapper. You're not getting it and that's final!"

Then the checkout clerk has the nerve to look at me as if to say, "Why aren't your children better behaved?"

I want to yell, "Because, you planned it this way!"

The tantrum tactics reach high gear in stores that

throw in a toy section. Shouldn't a drug store only carry drugs? I can see how health and beauty products could conceivably fit into the drug store, but toys? The children sniff them out like bloodhounds. It takes me forty-five minutes to buy a bottle of aspirin. And by then I really need one.

My, how I long for the days of do-nothing shopping.

THE TROUBLE WITH THE HEAD

~

*A*n unearthly wail broke the silence one morning. I followed the cry and found my son lying on the living room floor. The child was holding his right knee tightly with both hands and flailing from side to side.

"What happened? Are you all right?" I asked, dropping to the floor and frantically feeling for broken bones.

Still the child cried out, "It hurts! Owie! Owie!"

Rolling up his pant leg revealed the beginnings of a large bruise on his knee. The poor dear. He was obviously suffering. I ran around the house collecting pain-relieving paraphernalia.

I carried the child to the couch and slipped a downy pillow under his neck to gently cradle his head and another under the damaged limb. On top of the knee, I placed a cold pack to keep the swelling down. I counted out the maximum number of pain reliever tablets for a child his age and watched with anxiety as he chomped on the chewables. With a prayer on my lips, I bathed his forehead with a cool cloth. To keep his spirits up I whispered plans for better days ahead, silently hoping there truly would be happy times again when this crisis had passed.

Then his older brother walked into the room--looking a tad smug, I might add.

"It's all his fault!" the wounded child wailed at the top of his young lungs. With what little strength remained, he raised his hand. His finger quivered as it pointed out the guilty party.

"What have you done to him?" I demanded.

"Nothing," the viscous one replied.

"What do you mean, 'nothing'? Just look at your brother!"

The injured one groaned pitifully. It seemed to be a struggle for him to keep his eyes open. He reached out for my hand.

I held the poor suffering creature in my arms. Then I addressed the inflictor of the wounds. "Tell me what evil you have done!"

"Okay Mom," the confession began. "I have to admit it. I guess I just have too hard a head."

"Your head? What were you doing? Ramming the poor kid?"

"No. He kneed me in the forehead."

"Yea!" yelled the injured party with amazing rejuvenation. "He just stood there and let me do it."

"If I had quicker reflexes, I would have moved. Believe me."

"Well Mom, what is he doing with such a hard head in the first place? If his head wasn't so hard my knee wouldn't be hurting so much now," reasoned the younger boy.

I said, "Yes what a pity a skull is so hard! If the brain weren't so wimpy, and in need of such thick protection, kneeing someone in the head could be a completely painless experience. The knee would sink into the marshmallow-like substance and bounce back almost unscathed. Those hard heads are truly to blame. If you don't live through this little incident, you'll have to speak to someone on the 'other side' about this." I whipped the pillow out from under his head. It was hard enough to take it.

LEWIS AND CLARK DIDN'T HAVE
KIDS ALONG

~

*W*hat's your favorite genre? Mysteries, romance, suspense, horror, science fiction? My husband's is maps. He sits up with a good map into the wee hours of the morning. He just can't put it down.

Like a favorite book that gets better every time you read it, my husband relives past vacations as he goes down memory lanes and memory highways. "Remember when we were going to camp that night right here," he says waking me from a sound sleep.

He chuckles uncontrollably, "It was pouring. You were such a worrier. You were sure we'd be hit by lightning, like we were all walking around with lightning rods on our heads or something. People do camp in the rain you know. The rip wouldn't have let in much water. And that old tree that burst into flames was nothing to get all worked up about. But I kept driving," he says, pointing, "down here, then on to this little grey road. It sure doesn't look like a gravel road on the map. Does it?"

I struggle to focus my eyes in my dream state. "Nope. It looks like a smudge mark."

"And there's that turn I missed. So that's how we got clear over here. I wonder how those farmers managed with no gas station for 270 miles."

"Yes, that was a long night, wasn't it?"

"But this year will be different," he vows as he shows me his plans for the current trek.

"I don't know, it looks like it's starting to be a long night already," I mutter. My eyes glaze over as he details taking an extra day for this and a few extra miles to see that. I try not to wince as he speaks of little side roads that would cut off all the unnecessary scenery and major city centers. I even try not to look suicidal as he speaks of extra camping stops.

Who decided camping was a form of recreation, I'd like to know? Don't we have modern conveniences for a reason? Party pooper that I am, I happen to enjoy sleeping in a bed. Sleeping bags seem comfy enough until you lay one out over raised tree roots and try to get a little shuteye. Babies happen to agree with me...for hours on end...at high decibels! (I have seen many a wonderful sunrise due to children who rebel against the great outdoors.)

Tell me, why would we shun the boons of civilization and strike out into bear-infested wilderness to get away from it all? We haven't even left yet and I can hardly wait to get back to it all.

My husband claims this year will be different. It won't be any different. In fact, I'm quite sure it will be worse. Not only do we have a one-year-old, who balks if her mobile doesn't have the puppy facing north, we've invited some friends along. My husband wants to plan a really good time for them...I hope we live through it.

PART III

A QUIET, BLISSFUL MOMENT

ALONE IN THE CAR

~

I was alone in the car. It was a novel experience. I drove for five minutes before I realized I was listening to the kiddie music. I switched to the radio. After listening for a few minutes, I realized I didn't know any of the words to the songs, except for re-recorded versions of disco greats (which was about half of them).

What happened to me? I am no longer hip. Instead, I'm just hippy. No one can tell hip size in a car, however. No one can tell what song I've got playing in the car, either. So I put the kiddie songs back on.

I sang out loud. I was really jammin'. "Twinkle, twinkle little star " was never so cool. At a stoplight, the steering wheel became a drum. The drum solo in "I'm a little teapot" is smokin'. Soon I got the windshield wipers into the act. They rocked back and forth precisely to the beat of "Bingo was his name-o." It was a mystical experience.

The crowd was going wild. Their arms in the air

mimicked the wipers as each person screamed for more. I pressed my mouth against the microphone, squinted into the sun, surveyed the tens of thousands in the outdoor stadium, and said, "Thank you! Thank you very much! For my next number, I'll do one of my personal favorites." The crowd waited with bated breath. I paused an extra moment for dramatic effect. Finally, I yelled into the microphone, "The wheels on the bus!"

The crowd could hardly contain their excitement. Big, strong, football player-types were fainting into their date's arms. Young girls were screaming and ripping at their hair. As I began to sing, a hush fell over the crowd. All those still conscious twirled their hands as I sang, "round and round." They stood "up and down" on cue, and chimed in for the other verses. Fans sat cross-legged on the stadium grass and swayed. Surely Woodstock would pale by comparison.

Amid the deafening applause of my encore, "Mary had a little lamb," I attempted my exit. The announcer thundered above the crowd, "Momma-Tunes has left the building." I waved from my baby blue limousine as people thrust autograph books at the window. I blew them a kiss.

Was that a blow horn? Were the policemen having trouble with crowd control? I looked out the window. A burly man in a truck hung his head out his window and yelled, "The light's green! Wake up!"

As I shook off the disorientation, I noticed the lady in the car beside me. Her mouth hung open and her eyes held an expression of wonder. Behind her car, there was a young man on a motorcycle. He was laughing so hard he had removed his helmet to wipe tears. Although I was alone in the car, my mind failed to register that I was not alone on the road. I felt isolated in the car but the truth is I was out in public jamming to "Eensy Weensy Spider" like there was no tomorrow. I'll never go anywhere without my kids again.

CONFESSIONS OF LITERARY REGRESSIONS

~

*T*he books we choose say a lot about us. I like to roam the genres. Mystery one day and romance the next. Fiction mingled with non-fiction makes for a balanced library. Recently, however, my tastes have taken an unusual turn. I am concerned.

The other night I reached over to my night table for a book to read. I found The Cat in the Hat by Dr. Seuss. I hate to admit that, but it gets worse. I couldn't find anything better to read, so I read it. The children had been asleep for hours. I have no alibi!

I enjoyed it so much I considered tiptoeing up to my daughter's bookshelf for Green Eggs and Ham. That's when I realized I had a problem. This wasn't my first literary regression, just the most severe.

Last summer I read The Hobbit by Tolkien to my older children. It took us a few weeks and the children really enjoyed it. Almost as much as I did. I was initiating the reading sessions as much as they were. As soon as there was a free moment, I was asking, "Who wants to find out if Bilbo gets away from the spiders?"

"But Mom we need to clean our rooms," they replied.

"Oh, never mind about that," I said. "We can't leave Bilbo and the dwarfs caught in those spiders' threads another minute." The suspense was killing me.

That was the beginning. From there, I have enjoyed literature aimed at increasingly decreasing age groups until now I enjoy most thoroughly the preschool picture book category. I hang out in the juvenile section of the library trying to talk my three-year-old into choosing books I want to read.

My readings are beginning to affect me. I believe in fairy godmothers and plan to go for a good cry in the backyard so one will show up and magically clean the basement for me. I notice a blemish and wonder if I may be the victim of a turning-into-a-frog curse. I watch for signs in the morning mirror (which I sometimes talk to). On airplanes with cranky babies, I'm sure I've spotted wicked witches and heard them say, "Stuff a sock in it, My Pretty."

I've been wondering if perhaps these sorts of things happen to all people when they become parents. Reading to children is great fun. The world of children's literature is not a world I want to leave behind.

So what if I loved Shakespeare in University. Who cares if the deep thinking of Henry David Thoreau used to interest me? My tastes are changing. In fact, I'm beginning to think that anybody who can read a whole chapter about a bean field in Walden has a dangerous surplus of time on his hands.

A GET-AWAY TO THE TIME-OUT SPA

I want to be a kid. I'm not jealous of their overflowing energy. Well, okay, maybe I'm a little jealous. I'm not envious of their hours of playtime, though. All right, I'm quite envious. Mostly what I want, though, is their punishment. I would thoroughly enjoy a getaway that included a full day of my child's basic discipline. I don't think I'm alone in this wish. There is a market to tap into here. I plan to one day open the first Time-Out Spa. The idea came one day when my daughter had been especially trying.

The child teased her younger sister. She was sent to her room. Then she hit her older brother. She had to sit on a chair for a time-out. She was the author of a new game involving screeching at the top of your lungs and jumping on beds and couches. She had to have quiet time during which she read a book and colored in her coloring books. As the day started to come to a close, she took out every game and began a mix and match party. I declared an early bedtime was in order. As I tucked her in, the summer sun was still high in the sky. She said, "I've had no fun today. How would you like it?" I thought about that. I decided that I would. In fact, I'd like it a lot!

At the Time-Out Spa, I will be sent to my room. I won't have concerns of earning a living or cleaning a house. I won't have to do any meal planning, bill paying or laundry. There will be no one else that I am responsible for during my get-away. I will only be required to go to my room for a little rest and relaxation. It will be mandatory. Anyone at the spa pouring over a calculator, a chequebook, or a daytimer will be promptly sent to her room.

Quiet time will be another favorite spa feature. During quiet time I will read to my heart's content. Maybe I'll play with my child's Quiet Book. That sounds heavenly. Then there will be time for creativity. For some patrons that may be coloring in coloring books, for others it may be painting, sketching, sculpting, writing, knitting, or other creative pursuits. Quiet time will be a joy.

Grounding will be a necessary component of the spa stay. You aren't allowed to leave during the length of your visit. Children who call up their mothers to drive them to soccer tournaments will be told, "Sorry, Honey. I'd like to get up at 5:30 to have you there for the 8:00 a.m. game but I'm grounded. I'm not allowed to leave. Dad will have to take you while I have my facial and wash behind my ears."

Instead of running from one task to another, participants at the Time-Out Spa who are feeling stressed will be sent to sit on a chair. A comfy, cozy chair where they can put up their feet and meditate. Then after a long day at the spa, they will enjoy the early bedtime. I may even sleep in.

There is, however, a danger that my behavior will

deteriorate. This punishment might be so good that I am bound to start acting up just for the attention.

SNOW: A MOTHER'S AND SON'S
PERSPECTIVE

~

" *H* ey look! It snowed last night! Isn't it great?"
the child gushed.

I went to the window. He was right. It was the first
week of October and snow was everywhere. It was
absolutely depressing.

"There are so many fun things to do with the snow,"
the little boy continued. "I can make snow-angels and
snowmen. We are so lucky to have so much snow already!"

I rolled my eyes. "Really lucky," I said. Now there are
walks to shovel. Now there are snowsuits to find and sets of
mittens to match. Boots with super-duper traction will soon
be dragging the entire snowfall into my living room. Soon
I'll be crawling around on my hands and knees trying to
gather the snow clumps left by super-duper traction before
they melt. Oh yes, there are so many fun things to do with
the snow.

My son struggled into his snow-frolicking wear. With

my help, he was all ready in twenty minutes. He said, "Winter coats are so toasty warm, aren't they?"

"They have to be," I said and closed the door behind him without further comment.

It was supposed to be fall. I had just bought a cute fall coat and I wore it twice. Twice, can you believe it? And now it was winter. We live in a place with two seasons: summer (for about fifteen minutes) and winter (the rest of the time). Spring and fall coats are a needless extravagance.

The door burst open. "Guess what I'm doing?" My son's face was beaming and his tongue was hanging out.

"Licking the doorknob?" I asked.

"No. I'm chasing snowflakes and catching them on my tongue. I've caught twenty-two!"

"Great. I hope they weren't made with acid rain," I said.

When catching snowflakes I, unfortunately, miss many more than I catch, and they're all over my hair in seconds. After two minutes in the warmth of a building, I look like someone has dumped a bucket of water over my head. I spend a long time on my hair, gelling, blow drying, and curling...well, okay I spend a couple of minutes, but that's beside the point... the snow flattens it, or worse...I put on a toque. Talk about a bad-hair season.

Seconds later the rosy-cheeked youngster stomped through the house yelling, "Mom, help me. My boot is stuck. It won't come off."

"Off? Don't take it off. You just got out there," I pleaded as I pushed the boot firmly back on his foot.

"It's cold out there."

"What about making snow angels?" I said, enthusiastically.

"I already did that."

"Snowmen! What about making snowmen? That's a blast!"

"Naw. I just want to come in."

"But Honey, I thought you said that there were so many fun things to do in the snow."

"It was fun, lots of fun. But now I'm bored. What do you want to do now?"

I sighed a long sigh. It was clear I wouldn't have a moment to myself again for the next eight months.

PART IV

TRANQUILLITY IS AN ILLUSION

THAT'S ABOUT THE SIZE OF IT

~

The radio was blaring as my four-year-old lounged on the couch, listening. In the same room, the keyboard was cranked to the max as my six-year-old created audio masterpieces. Neither child's activity seemed to bother the other. They were content to selectively listen to their own music.

I was in the shower. I was not content to listen to their mixture. The barrage on my eardrums was like an assault. A peaceful moment of silence (one of my few during the day) was ruined. Usually, time seems to stand still when I'm under a hot, steaming shower and all is right in the world. But in the midst of utopia, this noise began.

By the time I had my robe on, I was sure I was on the brink of a nervous breakdown. My thoughts were scattered, disoriented, and certainly, irrationally violent. The room was spinning, and my temples were throbbing wildly. *My brain is going to explode*, I thought.

My brain didn't explode. Once the silence returned,

the good ol' grey matter slowly seeped back into the recesses of the cranium, back to normal size. Or so I thought.

Later that day, I read an article in a ladies' magazine that was a real shocker. It appears that things are worse than I suspected. The article claimed that scientists have discovered that stress can damage your brain...even cause it to shrink.

So the pain in my temples wasn't from swelling, it was actually from shrinking. My heavens, do I have anything left? I have five little kids. I've been up in the middle of the night with colicky babies. I have had children with ear infections, bumped heads, bruised knees, broken legs, high fevers, unexplained vomiting and strange spots. I've worried about the sound of a cough, the color of mucus, the consistency of bowel movements. I've had decisions about whether or not to allow trick-or-treating candy to be eaten, which babysitters to trust, what movies to approve of, what a fair bedtime should be. I've spent so much time trying to be a peacemaker that I should get an honorary doctorate degree in labor relations. My life has not been void of stress!

I've been trying on old hats to see if they seem any looser. I've tried knocking on the top of my head to see if it sounds noticeably more hollow up there. Yesterday my husband saw me lying on the bathroom floor with my head on the scale. "Have you lost your mind?" he asked.

"Well, not all of it," I said.

I have no concrete results from my studies, but I don't mind telling you, I'm worried. I forget what time common events occur, like church meetings, school bells, and clubs I have been a member of for two years. In the middle of a heated debate with my eight-year-old, I forget the child's name, trying out each of the other children's names before finally getting it right. My purse, keys, and hairbrush have all grown legs. It is blatantly obvious that at the present rate of consumption, I'll use up my last brain cell sometime around the middle of next month.

Don't get me wrong. I'm not complaining. Once my mind is used up, I'll be completely stress-free! I can hardly wait!

DESIGNING A QUIET AFTERNOON

~

The six-year-old child met her dad at the door.
"Shh. Be very quiet."

"What's the matter?"

"Shh, I said. Tiptoe through the living room."

"Is Mom sick? Why is shy lying on the couch?"

"She's sleeping. Come in the kitchen and I'll tell you all about it."

The child led her father to the table, got out a glass and placed it in front of him. Then she brought the milk and two cookies on a plate. "Make yourself comfortable, it's a long story."

He bit into one of the cookies and with a smile on his face said, "Okay Sweetie, tell me all about it."

"Okay. It all started with the sunshine."

"You don't say."

"It was such a beautiful day that Mom decided we should go for a picnic at lunch time. She was very excited about it. She packed the picnic basket with all the yummy foods in the house. She even wanted to bring the ice-cream but I told her we should wait until later for that because it might melt."

"Good thinking."

"I know. Mom usually thinks of these things, but she was so hyper about the picnic she must've forgot. She said she wanted to picnic at a park with slides, merry-go-rounds, and lots of stuff to climb on. We had lots of energy to burn off and she wanted to have a quiet afternoon."

"It looks like it worked."

"She *has* been resting peacefully. I think this is the best nap she's had in a long time. And it's no wonder. At the park, she played really hard. She helped the baby go down the slide about a million times. Mom wanted to race to everything, too. 'Let's race to the merry-go-round.' 'I bet I'll be the first one to the slide.' She kept making the baby run around. It was so weird. We could hardly get Mom to sit still long enough to eat her sandwich. She just wanted to play, play, play."

"How did you ever get her to come home?"

"It wasn't easy. We had to threaten to leave her there on the swing all night long. When I took her keys and got in the driver's seat, she finally came. She got in the car and said, 'I think everyone is ready for a nap now, don't you?' But Dad, she was the only one who was ready. She lay on the couch with the baby and was asleep in seconds. Soon the baby was up playing around but Mom didn't even notice. She was too sleepy."

"Poor Mom."

"I just hope that after this long nap she'll be able to go to sleep tonight. I don't want her up half the night. I'm tired."

MYSTERIOUS EVENING ILLNESSES

~

*P*erfectly healthy children undergo an unusual transformation when bedtime rolls around. Nobody requires medical attention in the morning. Never are there complaints of suffering while they are playing in the sandbox at noon. However, right after that final teeth-brushing ritual, the ailments come in full force.

There are four major illnesses that plague our home from the moment "bedtime" is uttered until sleep mercifully claims the children for a few precious hours of reprieve. Every parent has seen the symptoms, yet I can't find a cure in any medical journal.

1) Reoccurring Thirst Disease

My poor children are perpetually dehydrated through the evening hours. They come down for a drink, have a refreshing cool one, and before they've reached the top stair they are heading back down for another. Their thirst is unquenchable. You'd think our glasses are thimble-size, the way they act. A child who plays in the summer sun with only one drink break all afternoon needs seven drinks in ten minutes at bedtime. What kind of insidious disease is this? They can't go to bed. They have to stay up, close to the taps.

2) After Tennis Elbow

In the middle of a sport, my children feel no pain. Afterwards, much longer afterwards, they are in all sorts of pain. This goes beyond the adrenaline rush that can accompany physical activity. This is weird.

During a family soccer game, the children slide, fall, and break fingernails, all without complaint. Then we go in for dinner; still, they are fine. They read a book; no pain results. They get ready for bed; pain overcomes them! The children develop delayed agony relating to skinned knees, bumped elbows, and hangnails. It is unbearable. They can't be expected to go to bed in this kind of condition. They need all sorts of healing attention.

3) The New Chicken Pox

This illness is also known as the scaredy cat syndrome. My children become scared of any number of things after they have been sent to bed. Often the reason for the fear cannot even be pinpointed. "I'm just scared," is all the child can say.

I have sometimes compounded the problem by asking, "Well, what is there to be afraid of?" This only sets the child's imagination off and running. "Well, there could be a fire. There could be a robber. There could be a rat the size of an elephant trying to eat my brain." That scares me. And the child and I stay up together.

4) Bed Head Aches

Headaches come in epidemic proportions at bedtime. It's the quiet, I think. Children simply cannot tolerate the quiet. That's why they play loud games of make-believe;

they like the racket. That's why they get into arguments with each other; they need to hear yelling. That's why they play their music loud enough to rattle light fixtures; it soothes them. So, when bedtime comes and they are tortured with silence they can't take it; it's headache city.

I fear the strange evening illnesses are here to stay. There is no vaccine to protect against them. There is no medicine to combat them. The only cure would be to eliminate bedtime altogether and that would lead to mysterious evening mental illnesses in parents.

A LETTER TO MY TRAVEL AGENT

~

*M*y dear sweet travel agent:

My opening salutation may seem a bit forward, seeing as how we have never met, but if you will let me explain, I think you will understand. You are about to become my dearest friend. I need a vacation. I'm sure, in your line of work, you hear that sentence a lot. I'm writing to tell you...No, I *really* need a vacation.

Some people get long weekends away from their work. On long weekends, my work increases. There are more people messing up the house all day long. More traipsing over the floors, more fingers sliding along the walls. Dirty is on speed dial.

Other people enjoy summer vacations. On summer vacations I have to pack for my children and plan for all the variations in the weather. The packing requirements for a one-year-old, alone, could prompt many a sane person to consider renting a U-Haul. So, typical vacations will not do. I need a real break.

As for the destination of my vacation, I have a few requirements you will need to know. They are very important and should not be overlooked when you are planning my get-away. I want to go somewhere where there are the following luxuries:

-Everyone can cut his own meat

-I can walk about freely without someone clinging to my lower leg

-I can cross my legs without someone climbing aboard for a horsy ride

-I can eat lunch at one thirty, if I am so inclined

-I am allowed to recline, and stay so inclined for a long time

-Everyone can pour his own cereal, and no one wants cereal before 8:00 a.m.

-I can do aerobics without watching for little fingers.

-I can go to the library without snarling, "Settle down! You are not in a jungle gym!"

-I can sit in a waiting room without a truckload of toys and little snacks in zip-lock baggies

-Nobody tells me, "I made a fluff."

-Everyone can drink without spilling

-I won't have to tie anybody's shoes, even my own

-Nobody wants praise for remembering to flush

-I can enter a restaurant without bussing staff fighting about whose section I will be seated in

-Nobody cries because the Nintendo game didn't save properly

-Nobody cries because her socks have lost their elasticity and hang around her ankles

-Nobody cries and then wipes his nose on my shirt

-Nobody cries because his tropical drink didn't come in the *red* glass

I know it's a tall order. But those are the bare necessities. I sincerely hope you can make the arrangements for my dream holiday.

*Y*our very good friend,
     Susan

P.S. My vacation will also need to include unconditional love and five little hugs both morning and night. I couldn't do without those.

P.P.S. Never mind. All I really need is a steamy hot bubble bath and I'll be rejuvenated for another day.

Dear Reader,

Thank you for reading Generation Why.

I hope you enjoyed it. If so, please leave a nice review on Amazon, Goodreads or wherever you hang out online.

And if you are in the trenches of raising children, I salute you and pray for an extra measure of patience and love to come your way.

Susan Bohnet

P.S. Visit susanbohnet.com for info about my other books, including Family Frenzi books in this series.

<<<<>>>>

www.ingramcontent.com/pod-product-compliance
Lightning Source LLC
Chambersburg PA
CBHW071632040426
42452CB00009B/1584